101 Ways to Motivate Your People

First Published in Great Britain in 2008
by NightHawk Publishing

All rights reserved

The right of Derek Owen to be identified as the author of this work has been asserted by him in accordance with the Copyright, Designs and Patents Act 1988.

This book is sold subject to the condition that no part of it, by way of trade or otherwise, be reproduced, lent, resold, hired out, stored in a retrieval system, or transmitted by any means, without the publisher's prior consent, in any form of binding or cover other than that in which it is published and without a similar condition being imposed on the subsequent purchaser.

A CIP catalogue record for this book is available from the British Library

ISBN 978-0-9559792-0-0

INTRODUCTION

This book is the result of the author's experience as a coach, consultant, manager and trainer over the last 25 years. It combines this experience with that of thousands of people attending personal development training and coaching events, from a wide range of different industries and at all levels of seniority.

There is no magical way to motivate people. However there are certain techniques and approaches that work well when applied in a flexible and personal way.
In this book you will discover 101 of these techniques and approaches, all designed to bring about positive increases in the motivation of other people.

At the end of this book there is a *'motivation at work questionnaire'*, and a scoring grid and interpretation guide, to help you identify what motivates you and your people at work.

Please feel free to contact me with any questions that you may have or to organise a 'Motivation' workshop.
Email: derek@skillsfx.com
To your success.

Derek Owen

AN OVERVIEW

MOTIVATION - That which causes action, reaction or inaction. It's the emotional driving force that results in certain actions and behaviours.

People are always motivated.......

It's just motivated to **DO WHAT !**

Some examples

A. A fire alarm goes off and we may be motivated to run, to collect our personal effects or to help others.

B. Our name is #1 in the sales figures and we are motivated to do anything to stay there.

C. Our child goes to their first school and we are motivated to leave work early every day to meet them.

D. An employee with 20 years service is motivated to sabotage the production line because of redundancy.

E. A usually communicative Manager who has been given unreasonable targets becomes a task master.

LET'S GET STARTED

1. Get to know what motivates people. Ask them and listen carefully to the answers that they give. How people communicate and express their feelings and thoughts will tell you how important certain things are to their personal motivation. Emphasis is often placed on these important areas through loudness, word selection, inflection, gestures, word stress, breathing, pauses, eye contact and other behaviour. Look and listen for clues. Spend time getting to know how each individual demonstrates their motivated and demotivated states. You now have a simple motivational measuring system.

2. Encourage people to identify and record what they think their personal motivators and drivers are. Ask people to identify times and events when they were both motivated and demotivated, and to think about the triggers and warning signs for these motivational states? What happened, why did they feel this way, what did they do and what was the impact and consequence of this. More importantly what do they need to do next time, to ensure that they identify these triggers early and have a plan to maintain motivation and neutralise demotivation. Ask what part you can play in this plan and support them in its implemetation.

3. Run a skills and knowledge induction programme for new starters or refresher training for existing staff. Lack of skills, knowledge or understanding can have a negative impact on motivation and may also increase levels of stress and absence.

4. Ensure that people do not become dependent on you for their personal motivation, otherwise when you are not around their motivation levels may drop. Their motivation is their responsibility, so consider adding this to individual job descriptions, objectives and appraisal systems. Congratulate and reward people for maintaining their motivation.

5. Develop your personal understanding of different motivational theories and approaches. There is no magic answer for increasing motivation, so it's important to have a range of tools and techniques and this helps to treat each person individually.

6. Ask questions and deliver immediate feedback when you observe people in a motivated state. Note what they are doing, how they are doing it and the results they get. Use these observations as feedback to encourage repetition of positive activities and behaviour. Giving positive feedback, along with evidence is also very motivational.

7. Know what motivates you and ensure that you personally remain motivationally balanced and calm at all times. Changes in your motivation levels will be picked up by others and can influence their motivational states. As a leader and manager of people it is important that you show a consistent emotional state. This way people will feel confident in you and will be motivated by your naturally balanced, calm and reflective leadership approach.

8. Recruit people into the team who have personal qualities, characteristics and mindsets that will compliment the existing team and not cause a rift. Communicate the recruitment process to everyone concerned and consider involving the team in either part or all of the recruitment process.

9. Ensure that everyone knows where and how they fit into the organisation, department and team, and that people know the importance of their role within the bigger picture. People often feel demotivated because they cannot see how their role makes a difference. It is important to regularly communicate and remind people of the significance and importance that their role has and why this is the case. Support this by giving real life examples and evidence of exactly what you mean.

10. Ensure that each role has an up-to-date job description and that this includes the skills, knowledge and behaviors required for that role. It is important that standards and expectations are detailed, as people feel more motivated when they have something to aim for, and know exactly what is expected from them.

11. Communicate the company, department and team vision and objectives on a regular basis and have these visible in a variety of different places within the company and department. This helps to build a positive team environment and shows how the team is playing its part in the bigger picture. Keep things fresh and alive by regular communication of successes and progress towards these objectives.

12. Involve people in the creation and development of the departmental and team vision and objectives. Hold regular meetings to discuss and review how things are progressing and encourage refinement of current plans and procedures. Communicate successes, identify shortfalls and concentrate on improvement solutions and actions. Avoid referring to just statistics or information and explain success in terms of what it means on the ground floor and what the benefits of this will be for everyone.

13. Discuss and agree with everyone how the team will work together, what is expected from each other, and the standards required from each individual. Agree what is acceptable and not acceptable within the team. Consider communicating these standards and this agreement in writing. Refer to these agreed standards if they are being exceeded or are not being achieved. This individual and team commitment helps create a team spirit, encourages individual responsibility, sets expectations and encourages people to achieve. It is also great for building a team atmosphere and team motivation.

14. Review team performance and standards on a regular basis. Discuss actual performance against target and identify successes and shortfalls. Agree what needs to continue, to start to happen, to not happen or requires adjusting. Discuss how the team is working together and the team agreement.

15. Communicate, monitor and review these agreed standards on a regular basis. Ensure they are still appropriate and that each individual is committed to them. Ask people how they are achieving these standards and use them as a feedback tool. *"Do you remember that you agreed that......... Well I have noticed that............"* (Achieving or not).

16. Discuss and agree with each person their goals objectives and targets. Encourage people to set there own and then agree and refine together. Ensure that these are written and are measurable, achievable, time bound, positive and reviewable. Include areas such as personal development, future career aspirations, pay and conditions, work load, teamwork, support needs, performance levels and standards and feedback processes.

17. Ensure that everyone understands what it is like to be a customer or client of your organisation. Get them to either experience this in real terms or to imagine what it might be like through role play. This is a very powerful exercise, helps to shift any negative mindsets and helps to develop personal empathy and understanding.

18. Review individual performance on a regular basis and discuss actual performance against targets. Gain their views first and identify successes and areas requiring development. Discuss areas such as training, targets, actual results, management information, personal goals and motivation levels. Agree a written personal action plan that includes what needs to continue to happen, to start to happen, to not happen or needs adjusting.

19. Identify the key information and activity data that it is important for you and your people to know to be able to monitor, review and evaluate processes, procedures and performance. Gain input and ideas from the team into what information they think it would be useful to capture and why. Get the team involved in the system as this will help to remove any fears that they might have in it.

20. Put in place a management information system that captures the key performance and activity data of what people do on a day-to-day basis. Review this regularly to ensure that it gives both you and the team all the information required to be able to make informed decisions regarding achievements, shortfalls and any development actions needed.

21. Communicate how the management information system works and discuss and agree the benefits of the system with everyone. EG. It helps focus resources in the right area, it identifies potential training needs, it improves communication and processes, it tracks trends over time and helps to identify shortfalls in systems, processes and procedures. Train and develop people in how to analyse, interpret and use the information in a positive and developmental way.

22. Analyse, interpret and use information as part of your leadership and management approach. Explain and demonstrate how this information is being used and the benefits of it. Explain that it's just part of the overall performance development equation and remove any potential fears, concerns or worries that people may have in the system. Encourage the team to analyse and interpret the information available and make recommendations.

23. Dig into what the management information and data might be telling you and track this over time. Identify trends and patterns and use the data as an indicator rather than as an absolute fact regarding what is happening. The data might be true but it is only as good as what it is, and how it is being captured. Dig deeply into the data to find out what it means and aim to get to the 'root cause'.

24. Get to know something about what your people do outside work. It is important not to pry into people's private lives, however an understanding of what else your people do is important, as this can help to build strong personal relationships. It provides you with alternative ideas for motivation and may also indicate possible external factors that could be influencing motivation at this moment in time.

25. Communicate openly, regularly and on an ongoing basis with your team and team members.

26. If there is nothing to communicate, communicate this, as it helps to prevent rumour and gossip.

27. Communicate using a variety of different methods and approaches. Vary your approach and consider using face to face, email, text, telephone, team meetings, posters, newsletters, weekly briefings, training, coaching, social and team activities etc.

28. Identify your own preferred communication style, as well as that of your people. (See, hear, feel) Develop your understanding of the different communication styles and how they react together. Develop your understanding of neuro linguistic programming (NLP).

29. Communicate using visual (see), auditory (hear) and feeling (feel) words. This will help to ensure that your communication is appropriate and right for the different communication styles that exist. It also helps to prevent individuals or groups from feeling isolated, disinterested and therefore potentially demotivated. It also helps to increase the effectiveness of your communication.

30. Ensure that you use positive language and words when communicating and avoid the use or overuse of words such as maybe, perhaps, might be, possibly, could be, should be, or like to think that etc. These words are not that positive. Consider replacing them with words such as will, can, when, we are, we will be, this will etc.

31. Identify and understand your behavioral style and that of your people. Behaviour is often a reflection of what people think and feel at a given moment in time and it is quite difficult to hide. Observing behaviour in people is useful for measuring and identifying their possible motivational state at any given moment in time. Adapting your approach to their style and needs increases understanding, rapport and empathy with that person and helps to increase their motivation level.

32. Identify and understand your personality type and that of your people. This will help you to understand how you come across to others and will provide you with the flexibility to be able to adapt your approach and style according to the situation and the type of person that you are communicating with. Again this understanding and adaptability will help to increase motivation levels.

33. Identify and understand your preferred team leadership style and approach. Different people are motivated by different team leadership styles. Knowing your preferred style and then having the flexibility to be able to adapt your approach is very important to motivation. This will also help you to understand the reasons why you are getting the results that you are currently getting. You can then plan a different strategy and approach, if needed.

34. Review and record the consequences and impact of your communication, behavioral and leadership style. Where and in what situations were and are these positive and motivational? Where are they not? Review these situations and create an action plan to develop the successes you have had, and to turn around any non motivational results you are getting. Commit to a few actions and review the results regularly.

35. Ask for evidence based feedback on your team leadership style. What works and what does not work for your people. Ask for examples of when this leadership style occurred and the impact that it had. Ask what could have been done differently and what impact this would have had. Commit to making these changes in the future and review.

36. Personally review your team leadership style and approach. Ask for, and review any feedback that you may already have received. Identify what you need to continue doing, stop doing, start doing and adjust. Create and write down a time bound personal development action plan, implement this, track the results you get and gain further feedback on how it is all going. Identify a mentor who has the qualities that you would like to develop and work with them in developing these.

37. Adjust your communication style, leadership style, and your behaviours according to the situation and the individual you are interacting with. Measure your success in real time and adapt your style and approach as required. Ask for feedback from the other person during your interaction with them and use this to fine tune your approach as required.

38. Hold regular one to one meetings to discuss and review business objectives, personal performance, targets, achievements, motivation levels, training, personal development, actions completed since the last meeting, improvement areas and potential solutions, news and other relevant areas. Ensure each meeting has purpose, is structured, uses time wisely, is focused on them and is benefit driven.

39. Ask people for feedback regarding the benefit that they receive from one to one meetings with you. Encourage open and honest feedback because if people are not receiving any benefit from them, then they need to be conducted in a different way, and you need to know this. Ask for ideas and suggestions as to how they would like them to be conducted and the reasons for this. Discuss and agree the areas where there will be change.

40. Communicate agendas prior to meetings, ask for any additional items that should to be included and involve attendees in setting the agenda, structure, content and format. Give others the responsibility for organising and running meetings, with you there for support if needed. This helps encourage personal responsibility and can lead to increases in personal satisfaction. Do not let them fail though.

41. Ask people to structure and run their own one to one meetings. It is their meeting, for their benefit and they should be involved in the process. A one to one should not be something that is done to someone. One to one meetings need to have value and be of benefit to all involved. Give balanced and positive feedback regarding how the meeting went and document agreed action plans.

42. Hold add hock informal meetings lasting for a few minutes to discuss how things are going in general and how people feel. No matter what kind of business you are in, most people have some level of feeling about their work and this influences motivation, behaviour and personal performance.

43. Hold regular team meetings and briefings using a variety of different approaches and formats. Vary the location, seating plans, speakers, use of audio and video, meeting activities, timing and duration and topics etc. Keep these meetings fresh and alive and get feedback from the attendees.

44. Give people responsibility for organising and running certain parts of meetings. Support them as required, observe and note what they do and give positive developmental feedback on how it went. This is motivational and keeps meetings fresh.

45. Hold regular team social events that cater for the needs of all attendee types. Take into account the personalities of those attending, physical abilities, age, size, sex, motivation, interests, affordability, outside influences such as family, eating and drinking needs, timing, getting home and security. Keep the events neutral and get feedback on them.

46. Deliver feedback in a positive and developmental way throughout the year. This feedback should be based on observed behaviour and should include the consequences and impact that this had on the situation. This feedback should be used as part of any annual appraisal system. Feedback should be immediate and there should be no surprises. EG. *"Remember 6 months ago when ………..''*

47. Give add hock positive feedback to support, encourage and motivate people. Focus on what you saw or heard and include the impact this had on things. Acknowledging and giving feedback in this way is motivational and helps in encouraging people to continue their positive behaviour.

48. Ask people for their thoughts on a situation prior to delivering your feedback. This will help you decide on the best feedback approach and the level of feedback to give. EG. If Bob says, *"This meeting was great, the customer knew exactly what I was offering"*, and you have evidence to the contrary, you might want to temper your feedback. People like giving their opinions and by asking them first, it enables them to vent their feelings and emotions about the situation which in turn helps to increase their receptivity to your feedback.

49. Consider avoiding the word feedback, as this word can stir up negative feelings, especially if there have been any negative feedback instances in the past. Words like *'Observations', 'How it's going'* or *'What I saw or heard'* could be used instead.

50. Ask people what benefit they derive from gaining feedback from you and what they think about the way you deliver this. Encourage openness and honesty, as any negative thoughts that people have about feedback will help you to adjust the way you deliver it. Feedback should have value and if people are not receiving this, then something needs to change. Communicate your view on the positive benefits of feedback and use success stories to support this.

51. Gain regular feedback, ideas and suggestions from other people. This might be about your leadership style, communication within the business, the work environment, processes and procedures or anything else. Listen carefully to any feedback given and ask probing questions for clarification. Ask for evidence, as feedback without evidence is just opinion. Summarise the feedback given, along with supporting evidence and use this to design solutions and action plans. Review regularly.

52. Gain feedback about the team from third party sources, such as customers and suppliers. Ensure that this feedback is communicated and that any negative feedback is tempered accordingly. Encourage people to initiate third party feedback themselves and get it in writing where appropriate.

53. Consider a suggestion box, communicate the ideas suggested and reward money saving or money making ideas. If an idea generates a saving of £200,000, a £45 bottle of champagne, or £50 of vouchers may not be that positive though!

54. Ensure that people have the skills, knowledge, understanding and tools required for the job. Put in place a structured training, development, coaching and support plan. Reward and communicate the skills and knowledge development that people have engaged in. Let people put their certificates on the walls or on their desks, if appropriate.

55. Implement a structured performance review and appraisal system and train people in how to use it. Ensure that the standards and requirements are fully documented and understood. Test the system prior to implementation and ensure that it's flexible, easy to use and supports the organisational goals.

56. Train people in how to identify, manage and deal with stress and stressful situations. Manage stress in a positive, personal and confidential way. People who are good with people often feel things more, which is why they're good with people. Supporting a stressed individual is very motivational.

57. Identify and understand the different learning styles and approaches that people have to learning and development. Take learning styles into account when running training events, development initiatives, coaching sessions and action plans. Avoid one learning approach for everyone, as this may be counterproductive and demotivational

58. Ensure that everyone has and owns an agreed written personal development plan and that they have a copy of this. This plan should be a living working document and should be discussed at one to one meetings and other development events.

59. Review personal development plans on a regular basis. Start by reviewing what actions have taken place since the last review, discuss, document and acknowledge successes and any shortfalls. Keep development plans manageable by focusing on just a few key development areas at any one time.

60. Discuss career development plans and aspirations as part of one to one meetings. Encourage people to develop their careers internally and externally. If an individual wishes to leave the business in 2 years time, it is better to have them motivated and committed for this time, performing well, rather than disengaged and demotivated.

61. Post individual and team successes in noticeable places and refer to these regularly. Consider changing the style of this communication so that it does not become the norm or lose its impact.

62. Ensure that the work environment is comfortable and appropriate for people's needs. Take into account things like seating, heating, water, phones, computers, coffee, lunch areas, relaxation zones, private access to the internet, showers, sports facilities, social clubs, personalising desks, parking and health and safety etc.

63. Encourage people to take regular rest breaks away from their desks and set aside a comfortable area where people can eat and relax. The ability for people to be able to recharge their batteries in a comfortable environment can be very beneficial for both personal performance and motivation.

64. Run regular team building events that are non work focused, varied and fun. This will help to build team relationships, team identity, team communication, and a sense of belonging and purpose.

65. Ensure there is consistency of approach within the team leadership and management teams and that coaching, feedback, appraisals, communication, one to ones and other leadership activities are run in a similar way and format. Lack of consistency can breed small talk, negativity, frustration and mistrust, which in turn can lead to demotivation and problems within the team.

66. Delegate responsibility to people who have the necessary skills, knowledge, desire, capability and motivation to get involved. Brief fully, ensure they have everything required to take this responsibility, agree review dates, deliver balanced ongoing feedback and acknowledge all areas of success. Be there as a coach to support, guide and assist.

67. Don't allow people to fail or become demotivated due to lack of leadership support, communication, coaching, training, planning, goal setting, personal development, tools and materials, feedback, skills, knowledge or understanding.

68. Build a solutions focused environment by asking people for their thoughts and ideas regarding options and solutions in specific areas. Do not ignore or put down other people's input. For some people it takes a lot of courage to bring an idea forward and any rebuff can be very demotivational. Deliver any developmental feedback delicately and on a one to one personal basis.

69. Organise and run an 'Improvement' forum that meets regularly to discuss improvement areas and ideas. Encourage input from everyone at all levels

70. Communicate improvement plans and the results of these to everyone on a regular basis. Review the 'Improvement' forum to ensure that it is working in the most effective way and gain feedback from everyone about how it is going.

71. Recognise and reward people according to their personal needs, the situation, their goals and what motivates them. Not everyone wants a holiday in the sun, especially if they are finding it difficult to make ends meet, because they have 2 hours travel to work by car and petrol costs more. Use this insider knowledge and reward people according to their personal situation and motivations.

72. Communicate with people daily and thank them on a regular basis. Lack of, or poor communication is often given as a contributing factor during exit interviews. Communicate personally, openly and on an individual basis whenever you can.

73. Deal quickly with poor performance in a structured, non emotional and positive way. Ensure that you document everything and seek expert advice if necessary. Do not allow it to impact negatively on the team and let them know what is happening without breaking confidentiality. Deliver balanced and constructive messages without opinion.

74. When communicating don't reveal personal or confidential information about others. Avoid taking sides, be impartial, balanced, fair, factual, non emotional, personal and decisive. Avoid giving too much information about your personal life.

75. Do not permit any individual to negatively effect or control the team or hold you to ransom, no matter what their level of personal performance, expertise, productivity or perceived influence and control they might have on the team. Discus with that individual the consequences of their continued behaviour and take the necessary action to resolve the situation.

76. Implement a variety of different competitions and games and gain feedback on those that work. Avoid running the same old competition every year and if a competition has finished give the results and prizes out quickly. Remove any banners and competition posters and then focus on the future.

77. Put the right people in the right job role at the right time for the benefit of them, the team and the business. EG. Analytical people may not be best suited for a think-on-your-feet type of sales or live complaint handling role and go-getting, I get bored quickly people, may not be best suited for a 3 month statistical analysis and reporting job role.

78. Do what you say you will do, when and how you said you would do it. Keeping to your word is vital and you only have to not do this once, for people to start not believing in you and mistrusting you. This can be very demotivational and negative.

79. If you are unable to do what you said you would do, explain the genuine reasons why as soon as possible. Tell the truth, as people can often see through any lies and may no longer trust or believe in you. They may not tell you that they know the truth, but their behaviour will demonstrate this.

80. Take notes and remember what has been agreed with people and refer back these notes. Do not manage by process, just remember that details and facts are important. EG. *"At our last one to one you said that you would ……… Please explain the reasons why you have been unable to do this?"*

81. Remember people's personal information such as children's names, birthdays etc. respect privacy but demonstrate that you have a personal approach to leadership by using this information in a natural and appropriate way. This can make a significant positive difference to relationships and individual motivation levels, but must be natural and genuine.

82. Manage each team member individually but apply a consistent and structured approach. Do not have favourites either real or perceived. EG. A team leader who invites a team member to their house because that person has personal problems, may create a lot of negative gossip and cause that team member to be isolated by the rest of the team.

83. Ensure that your suppliers adopt the same standards and behaviours that you have agreed as a team and do not allow them to get away with things that the team would not get away with.

84. Encourage people to relax and vent their stress and frustration through sport, activities, games and ongoing communication and feedback with both you and each other. Create a solutions culture.

85. Demonstrate that you are supportive and available if people want to talk to you. Have an open door policy and also a way of letting people know that you should not be disturbed at a particular moment in time, unless it is vital. Let the team know what is considered as *'vital'* and what the *'Do not disturb sign is'*. Review how this works and adjust.

86. Listen to new ideas with an open mind and do not dismiss anything in a negative way without hearing the whole story first. Watch your body language as you are listening to ideas, as this may give away your inner feelings. If you are unsure how to react, saying something mildly positive and then explain that you need to reflect on what has been said first, prior to giving a more comprehensive answer.

87. Post visual and audio motivational messages in key locations around the workplace. Get feedback from people and gain ideas and suggestions from managers. Keep these motivational messages and triggers fresh and alive by reviewing them.

88. Allow people to personalise their desks with appropriate decorations and objects, however take into account that what might be appropriate for one person might not be for another. Neutrality is the key and be particularly careful around allowing political and religious signs and symbols.

89. Reward people with something that is personal to them. Something that will last and be a positive and constant reminder of their success. EG. A diary, a keying for the car they aspire to own, a photo frame, a golf ball. Anything personal to them. This will help to reinforce positive behaviour, builds personal relationships and can lock in motivation.

90. Enjoy what you do, have fun in a natural, positive and professional way and **SMILE**. Motivation is contagious and if you are positive and motivated it will rub off on other people.

91. Focus on the benefits and positive outcomes that may result from a situation. Although it is important to acknowledge that a problem exists, there are always solutions and options to any situation. Explore these options together and communicate the positive benefits for everyone when things are resolved. Encourage people to focus on solutions.

92. Run regular skills practice events to develop new skills and to refine existing ones. Skills practice or role play is a great way of skills development in a safe environment and can be great fun and very motivational as well. Ensure that all scenarios used are realistic to at-work situations as this adds more credence and meaning to the skills exercises.

93. Implement a skills buddying or mentoring support system to develop and share skills within the team. Learning from each other and knowing that you have skills that someone else currently does not have is very motivational and is great for team building, communication and team relationships.

94. Trust people, give responsibility, allow ownership and if things do go wrong for any reason give them the benefit of doubt (once at least). To be trusted by someone is extremely motivational and positive.

95. Understand and appreciate that people are people and that mistakes can and do happen. It is the learning from these mistakes that enables personal growth and development. Working and supporting someone who has made a mistake sends a very strong message of belief and trust to that person.

96. Identify and capture 'best practice' within the team. Communicate this and ensure that people know where it originates from and who currently applies it Support and reward the application of 'best practice' and encourage its further development. Communicate and reward success.

97. Avoid changing your leadership approach and style too quickly, as the results of a previous change may not have had time to bear fruit. Remember that any change can be disconcerting, stressful, cause worry and be demotivational. So extra support, understanding and communication is important. Avoid too much change, too quickly.

98. Identify your values and beliefs and incorporate the appropriate ones into your leadership approach. Identify those that compliment the values and beliefs of both the organisation and individual team members. Get to know and understand people's beliefs and values, respect and support them.

99. Put your heart, energy, enthusiasm and passion into everything that you do. This can be very positive and motivational to other people and is contagious. Work this way with people, have their best interests at heart and motivation will follow.

100. Create a written action plan detailing the actions and activities that you will implement in order to increase the motivation levels of your people. Implement this plan, review it, adjust it where necessary and then re-implement. Keep doing this and improvement will follow.

101. Remember, if you always do what you always did, you'll always get what you always got and if this is not what was planned, then something has to be done differently!
So take massive positive action!

NUMBER 102

'Always give something a little bit extra, no matter how small'

IDENTIFYING WHAT MOTIVATES YOU AT WORK

This questionnaire will help you to identify what motivates you (or other people) at work. Look at the following 32 questions, on this page and score each statement using the scale below.

4 = Very important to me.	**3** = Quite important to me.
2 = Not important to me.	**1** = Not very important to me at all

THE FIRST 16 QUESTIONS

1	Having fun and enjoyment whilst I am at work	4	3	2	1
2	Feeling that I contribute to the organisation's success	4	3	2	1
3	Feeling that I have control of my own destiny	4	3	2	1
4	Having opportunities to socialise at work	4	3	2	1
5	Feeling that I am competent at my job	4	3	2	1
6	Succeeding at my work	4	3	2	1
7	Receiving encouragement	4	3	2	1
8	Being shown the significance of my work	4	3	2	1
9	Being asked for my thoughts and input	4	3	2	1
10	Being able to make choices at work	4	3	2	1
11	Being given responsibility for my work	4	3	2	1
12	Working in a team with a powerful identity	4	3	2	1
13	Using my hidden strengths and talents	4	3	2	1
14	Being allowed to set my own goals and objectives	4	3	2	1
15	Being shown appreciation	4	3	2	1
16	Knowing that what I do makes a difference	4	3	2	1

THE FINAL 16 QUESTIONS

4 = Very important to me.   **3** = Quite important to me.
2 = Not important to me.   **1** = Not very important to me at all

17	Having variety at work	4	3	2	1
18	Owning the work that I do	4	3	2	1
19	Being given leadership opportunities	4	3	2	1
20	Being a valued member of a team	4	3	2	1
21	Being given learning opportunities	4	3	2	1
22	Being encouraged to improve	4	3	2	1
23	Being recognised for my effort	4	3	2	1
24	Able to relate my objectives to the bigger picture	4	3	2	1
25	Feeling active and involved	4	3	2	1
26	Feeling responsible for what I do	4	3	2	1
27	Feeling empowered to make decisions	4	3	2	1
28	Feeling that I belong	4	3	2	1
29	Being able to learn through my mistakes	4	3	2	1
30	Being challenged to stretch my limits	4	3	2	1
31	Feeling rewarded for success	4	3	2	1
32	Having meaning from my job	4	3	2	1

SCORING GRID

Example score is in BOLD

Category	Question number	Question number	Question number	Question number	Category total
A	1 = 3	9 = 2	17 = 1	25 = 4	10

YOUR SCORE

Category	Question number	Question number	Question number	Question number	Category total
A	1 =	9 =	17 =	25 =	
B	2 =	10 =	18 =	26 =	
C	3 =	11 =	19 =	27 =	
D	4 =	12 =	20 =	28 =	
E	5 =	13 =	21 =	29 =	
F	6 =	14 =	22 =	30 =	
G	7 =	15 =	23 =	31 =	
H	8 =	16 =	24 =	32 =	

The maximum score in a category is **16**.

INTERPRETING YOUR SCORES

The higher the score the higher the potential influence that this area has on motivating you at work.

In which 2 categories did you score the **highest**?

Category =

Category =

The lower the score the less the potential influence that this area has on motivating you at work.

In which 2 categories did you score the **lowest**?

Category =

Category =

INTERPRETING YOUR SCORES

THE CATEGORIES

Category **A**:
Activity – being active and involved at work.

Category **B**:
Ownership – being able to own one's work.

Category **C**:
Empowerment – being empowered, taking control.

Category **D**:
Belonging – feeling part of a group.

Category **E**:
Competency – feeling able to use and develop one's skills.

Category **F**:
Achievement – feeling that goals are achieved.

Category **G**:
Recognition – being recognised for effort and success.

Category **H**:
Meaning – feeling that what you do has significance.

Final Thoughts

Motivation is like fingerprints. It is different and unique to each individual and what might motivate one person is unlikely to motivate another in the same way or to the same degree. In fact the opposite may be true.

Motivation within an individual is influenced by a range of different external factors, how these are interpreted and internalised, and the degree of importance that they have to them at any given moment in time.

To motivate an individual requires good understanding and communication with them, the ability to apply a range of different approaches and techniques, as well as regular monitoring and reviewing. Keeping things fresh and remembering that motivation has a sell by date is a very useful mindset to have.

One fact around motivation that has always stood out for me is the following:

The motivation of an individual is visible through their behaviour so it can be observed and measured. If you tune in to your people and communicate with them, you will discover how motivated they are and what it is that drives this motivation.

You then have 101 choices.

LEGAL NOTICE AND DISCLAIMER

There is no guarantee of success either written or implied and a variety of different factors need to be taken into account when working with and developing people. The author and/or publisher specifically disclaims any personal liability, loss, or risk incurred, as a consequence of acting on, undertaking or relaying on any advice or information presented herein. While all attempts have been made to verify the information provided in this publication, neither the author nor the publisher assumes any responsibility for errors, omissions or contradictory interpretation of the subject matter herein. This publication is not intended to be used as a source of legal or business advice. Please remember that the information contained may be subject to varying laws or regulations that may apply to the user's particular country and practice. The purchaser or reader of this publication assumes responsibility for the use of these materials and information. Adherence to all applicable laws and regulations, professional licensing, business practices, advertising and any other aspects of doing business within the country of residence of the reader or any other jurisdiction is the sole responsibility of the purchaser or reader.

The author and publisher of this publication assumes no responsibility or liability whatsoever as a result of reading and using these materials in anyway whatsoever. Any perceived slights regarding specific techniques, methodologies or ways of working are unintentional. Information contained within is provided solely for the user's information and, while thought to be accurate, is provided strictly "as is" and without warranty of any kind, either expressed or implied.

We will not be liable to you for any damages, direct or indirect, or lost profits or data arising out of your use of information provided. Every effort has been made to accurately represent our product, its potential, the benefits that can be derived from using it, when, where and how it can be used. Please remember that the success of each individual depends on a variety of different factors, including such things as background, dedication, desire, mindset, skills, knowledge, attitude and motivation.

www.ingramcontent.com/pod-product-compliance
Ingram Content Group UK Ltd.
Pitfield, Milton Keynes, MK11 3LW, UK
UKHW041433180426
11947UKWH00007B/410